Edinburgh Castle

CASTLES, Palaces & TOMBS

Scotland's Haunted Fortress

By Barbara Knox

Consultant: Stephen F. Brown, Director,
Institute of Medieval Philosophy and Theology, Boston College

BEARPORT
PUBLISHING

New York, New York

Credits

Cover and title page, © Patrick Ward/CORBIS; Pages 4-5 (both), © BRIAN HARRIS/Alamy; 6,
© Jeff J Mitchell/Getty Images; 7, © Philippa Lewis; Edifice/CORBIS; 8, © Dmitri Kessel/Time
& Life Pictures/Getty Images; 9, © Historic Scotland Photographic Library; 10, © Imagebroker/
Alamy; 11, © Worldwide Picture Library/Alamy; 12, © The Granger Collection, New York; 14,
© Steve Vidler/SuperStock; 15, © The Granger Collection, New York; 16, © Bettmann/CORBIS;
17, © The Granger Collection, New York; 18-19 (both), © www.undiscoveredscotland.co.uk; 20,
© VisitScotland/SCOTTISH VIEWPOINT; 21, © The Granger Collection, New York; 22,
© Craig Brown/Alamy; 23, © Worldwide Picture Library/Alamy; 24, © Mary Evans Picture Library/
Alamy; 25, © AP Photo/Chris Bacon; 26, © Justin Kase/Alamy; 26-27 (both), Graham White; 29,
Stephen Saks Photography/Alamy.

Publisher: Kenn Goin
Project Editor: Lisa Wiseman
Creative Director: Spencer Brinker
Original Design: Dawn Beard Creative and Triesta Hall of Blu-Design

Library of Congress Cataloging-in-Publication Data

Knox, Barbara.
  Edinburgh Castle : Scotland's haunted fortress / by Barbara Knox.
    p. cm. — (Castles, palaces & tombs)
  Includes bibliographical references and index.
  ISBN-13: 978-1-59716-248-7 (lib. bdg.)
  ISBN-10: 1-59716-248-5 (lib. bdg.)
  ISBN-13: 978-1-59716-276-0 (pbk.)
  ISBN-10: 1-59716-276-0 (pbk.)
  1. Edinburgh Castle (Edinburgh, Scotland)—Juvenile literature. 2. Edinburgh (Scotland)—
Buildings, structures, etc.—Juvenile literature. 3. Castles—Scotland—Edinburgh—History—
Juvenile literature. I. Title. II. Series.

DA890.E4C335 2007
941.3'4—dc22

2006011540

For more information, write to Bearport Publishing Company, Inc., 101 Fifth Avenue, Suite 6R,
New York, New York 10003. Printed in the United States of America.

10 9 8 7 6 5 4 3 2 1

Table of Contents

A Midnight Ghost

The **soldier** shivered in the cold, dark night. He was standing guard on Edinburgh Castle's highest wall, watching for the enemy. At midnight his **shift** would be over.

Suddenly, the sound of a drum cut through the stillness. *Dum, dum, dum de dum*. The hollow noise echoed across the castle's courtyard as it came closer and closer.

Gripping his sword tightly, the guard peered into the darkness. A young drummer marched slowly into view. As the boy stepped from the shadows, the guard gasped in horror. The drummer had no head!

Edinburgh Castle is located in the city of Edinburgh, the capital of Scotland.

The **legend** of the ghost drummer dates back to 1650. According to castle **lore**, the headless drummer appeared just before a battle.

A Fortress

Edinburgh Castle sits up high on an **extinct** volcano. **Historians** believe that people first settled on the rocky hill around 900 B.C. At first, a few round houses were built. Over time, they were torn down and other buildings were added. The castle has been used as a hunting cabin, a home for royals, a storehouse, and even a prison.

Scottish soldiers attend a ceremony at Edinburgh Castle in 2006

Towering 300 feet (91 m) above the city helped make the castle a strong **fortress**. Soldiers could see the enemy coming from miles (km) away. The rocky walls surrounding the castle were almost impossible to climb. Enemy soldiers had a hard time making their way up the steep sides.

One of the steep, rocky walls leading up to the castle

Today the castle is a working military base. It houses the Scottish division of the British **Army**.

A Haunted Castle

Edinburgh Castle is considered one of the most haunted places in Scotland. Even today, visitors report seeing ghosts. Many have felt invisible hands grab them. Others say they've felt the air suddenly turn ice cold, even on the hottest of days.

The ghost piper is another of the castle's famous ghosts. When alive, the piper played bagpipes in the tunnels beneath the castle. Then one day he disappeared and was never seen again. Today, some tourists claim to still hear his music.

Some people think that the beautiful Lady Jane Douglas still haunts the castle's grounds. In 1537, the king accused her of being a witch and put her in prison. Soon, soldiers dragged Jane outside and tied her to a **stake**. Then they burned her to death. Ever since, people say they can sometimes hear Jane crying.

The Castle Vaults were used as a prison starting in 1757.

Malcolm and Margaret

Malcolm the Third was the first of many **fierce** kings who lived in the castle. His dream was to take over northern England. He often led his army into battle against the English. He ordered his soldiers to burn their villages and kill the **peasants**.

Malcolm the Third and Queen Margaret give money to the poor people of Edinburgh.

In 1067, Malcolm met Princess Margaret and they soon married. Unlike Malcolm, Margaret was gentle and kind. The people of Edinburgh loved their queen.

Malcolm was killed in a bloody battle in 1093. Margaret died four days later. In her honor, their son built a **chapel** and named it St. Margaret's. He wanted everyone to remember his mother's kindness.

St. Margaret's Chapel is the oldest building in the castle. It's also considered the oldest building in the city of Edinburgh.

Most people who lived in Malcolm's time could not read or write. Margaret, however, loved to read and had many books.

Scotland at War

Like Malcolm, many other Scottish kings fought with the English. They led great armies into England to try to steal English land.

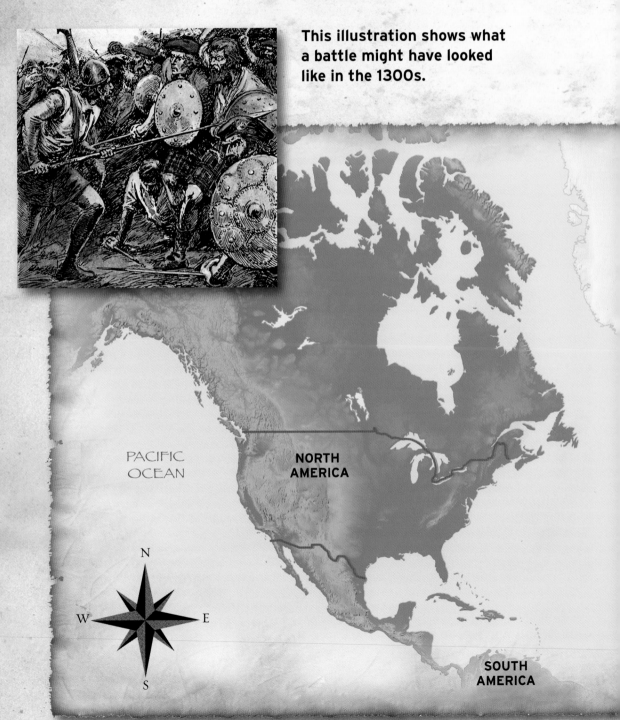

This illustration shows what a battle might have looked like in the 1300s.

PACIFIC OCEAN

NORTH AMERICA

N
W   E
S

SOUTH AMERICA

Some historians believe that the king's soldiers wore **kilts** into battle. They also carried heavy swords. Even the strongest men had to use two hands to handle the weapons.

Young boys also traveled with the army. They carried supplies such as spears, food, and clothing.

The huge army spread out for miles (km) as the men marched across the land. In 1296, the English and Scottish fought a great battle at Dunbar. When it was over, 10,000 Scottish soldiers lay dead.

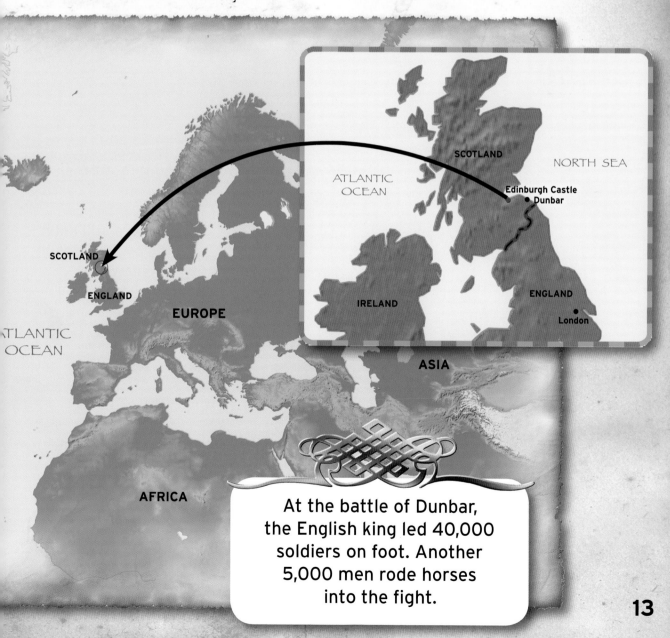

At the battle of Dunbar, the English king led 40,000 soldiers on foot. Another 5,000 men rode horses into the fight.

A Daring Attack

After their success at Dunbar, the English attacked the castle. Soldiers rammed the building with huge logs. Soon the doors crashed open. The soldiers ran inside and killed everyone in sight.

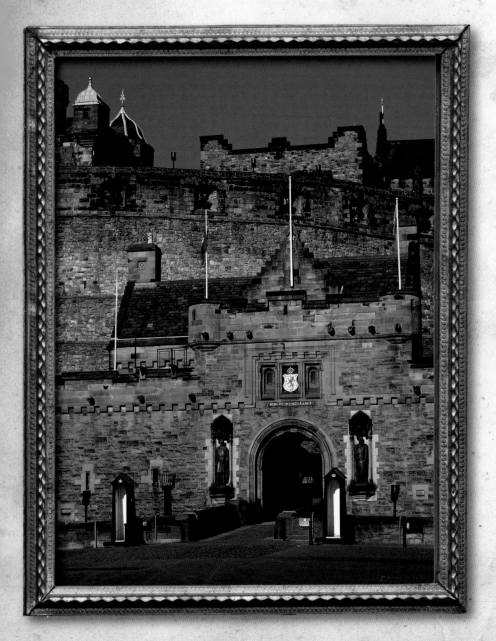

The Gatehouse was built in 1888 and became the castle's main entrance. Visitors still enter the castle through it today.

The Scots were determined to get their castle back. In 1314, Sir Thomas Randolph led 30 men on a surprise attack. The night was dark and still. The soldiers slowly climbed the steep rocks up to the castle. Then they used ropes to **scale** the castle wall. Quietly, they slipped over the top and surprised the English soldiers. After the battle, Edinburgh Castle once again belonged to the Scots.

Sir Thomas Randolph and his men scale the castle wall in 1314.

After Sir Randolph captured the castle, he destroyed most of the buildings. He believed if the castle were torn down, the English wouldn't fight to get it back. The buildings were not replaced for almost 50 years.

Siege!

Throughout the history of the castle, different armies have laid **siege** against it. A siege could last months or even years.

In 1571, thousands of English soldiers camped outside the castle. They used giant **catapults** to fling rocks as big as boulders at the Scots. The Scots fought back with arrows. They also shot rocks down onto the English.

This illustration shows what a siege might have looked like in the 1500s.

The siege lasted two years. During this time, the castle walls started to crumble. In the end, the English succeeded in completely knocking down one wall. Afterward, they ran inside and captured the Scots' leader, Sir William Kirkcaldy. Later, they chopped off his head.

Sir William Kirkcaldy

Most castles had murder holes carved into the walls. Soldiers poured boiling tar or water through these holes onto the enemy. The victims died slow, painful deaths from the burns.

Life in the Castle

Life in the castle was often crowded. Servants and soldiers lived there along with the royal family. Unlike most of the people in the castle, however, the king and queen lived well. They were waited on by the servants and slept in comfortable rooms. The other people slept on the cold stone floor.

Laich Hall was built in the 1600s and is part of the Royal Palace.

Everyone, though, gathered in the Great Hall for meals. A crackling fire warmed the room on chilly days. Servants brought the main meal to the table at 10 a.m. Dogs roamed the room while everyone ate. Some people tossed scraps of meat to the animals. Soldiers yelled to one another and spilled their drinks. The Great Hall was often noisy, smelly, and dirty.

The Great Hall was used for many things besides eating meals. Ceremonies were often held there, and, at one time, soldiers used the room for sleeping.

Until 1639, the Great Hall was also where the Scottish **Parliament** met.

A Time of Peace

In 1689, the fighting finally ended at Edinburgh Castle. Soldiers laid down their swords. Peace had come to the castle at last.

The Scottish government decided to unite with England in 1707. The rule of kings and queens in Scotland was over.

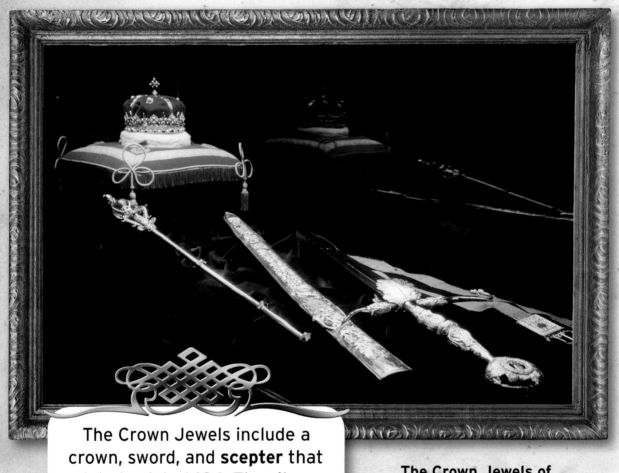

The Crown Jewels include a crown, sword, and **scepter** that date back to 1494. The silver sword stands four-and-a-half feet (1.4 m) tall. This height is taller than an average ten-year-old child!

The Crown Jewels of Scotland are also called the Honors of Scotland.

Servants packed up Scotland's Crown Jewels and stored them in a trunk in the Crown Room. For more than 100 years, everyone forgot about the jewels. Then in 1818, Sir Walter Scott, the famous author, discovered them in the castle. The jewels were put on display and they can still be seen today.

Sir Walter Scott

The Mighty Guns

The sound of gunfire has never completely left Edinburgh Castle. Since 1861, **gunners** have fired a **cannon** each day at exactly one o'clock in the afternoon. The sound helps everyone in the city know the correct time.

The One O'Clock Gun being fired

One of the most famous guns at the castle is called Mons Meg. It was given to King James the Second of Scotland in 1457. It took 100 men to move this mighty gun. Mons Meg was so powerful it could shoot a cannon stone more than two miles (3 km)! However, because of its heavy weight it was very hard to move around. The gun was last fired in 1680 to celebrate the birthday of King James the Seventh of Scotland.

Today, Mons Meg sits next to St. Margaret's Chapel.

English soldiers took Mons Meg to London, England, in 1754. It was displayed at the Tower of London and wasn't returned to the castle until 1829.

A Stone of Freedom

One of the castle's greatest treasures is the Stone of **Destiny**. This special rock stands for Scottish freedom.

Legend says that a man named Jacob used the red sandstone as a pillow more than 2,000 years ago. Travelers then brought it to Scotland around the year 850. Scottish kings sat on the stone when they were crowned.

For a time, the Stone of Destiny was placed under a throne at Westminster Abbey in London. Royalty sat above the stone while being crowned.

In 1296, an English king stole the stone and took it to London. Scottish soldiers tried to get it back. The stone, however, stayed in England for 700 years. In 1996, England's Prince Andrew finally returned it to Scotland.

During a ceremony in the Great Hall, Prince Andrew gave back the Stone of Destiny to Scotland. It is now on display in the Crown Room along with the Crown Jewels.

In 1950, the stone was stolen again. This time some Scottish students took it from the English. The stone was found three months later and returned.

Visiting Edinburgh Castle

More than one million people visit this haunted fortress every year. On their way to the castle, visitors can walk through the city of Edinburgh. They can stop and see historic sites such as the Sir Walter Scott monument.

Sir Walter Scott Monument

Castle Vaults

Great Hall

Royal Palace
(Includes Laich Hall
and the Crown Room)

Gate House

Once at the castle, they can look out onto the city. Beyond the city, the blue water of the North Sea sparkles in the sunlight. Visitors can then take a tour of the castle and learn about its bloody past and the mighty kings who once ruled Scotland.

St. Margaret's Chapel

Mons Meg

One O'Clock Gun

The people of Edinburgh speak English and Gaelic, an ancient language used by the Scots, Welsh, and Irish.

Just the Facts

- Scotland is one of four countries that make up the United Kingdom (UK). The other three countries in the UK are England, Wales, and Northern Ireland.

- Haggis is a traditional Scottish dish. It is made of sheep lungs, hearts, and livers, mixed with onions and oatmeal. Everything is cooked together in the lining of a sheep's stomach.

- Malcolm the Third's father was killed by Macbeth. William Shakespeare wrote a famous play called *Macbeth* in the early 1600s.

- In 1058, Malcolm the Third became the king of Scotland. He sat on the Stone of Destiny when he received the crown.

- On July 16, 2005, a lucky group of children went to Edinburgh Castle to hear author J. K. Rowling read from her book *Harry Potter and the Half-Blood Prince*. The next night, the children gathered in the castle for dinner in a room decorated to look like the Hogwarts' dining hall. Food was even served on golden plates.

Timeline

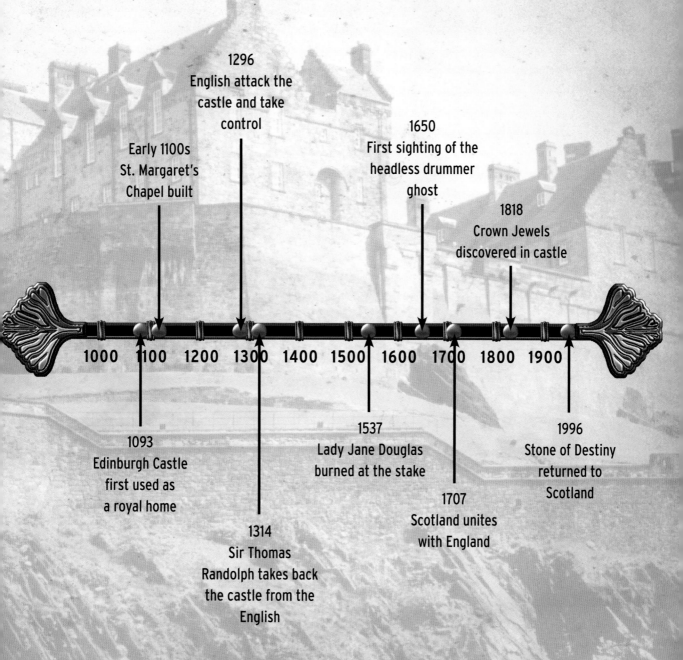

Early 1100s
St. Margaret's
Chapel built

1296
English attack the
castle and take
control

1650
First sighting of the
headless drummer
ghost

1818
Crown Jewels
discovered in castle

1000   1100   1200   1300   1400   1500   1600   1700   1800   1900

1093
Edinburgh Castle
first used as
a royal home

1314
Sir Thomas
Randolph takes back
the castle from the
English

1537
Lady Jane Douglas
burned at the stake

1707
Scotland unites
with England

1996
Stone of Destiny
returned to
Scotland

Glossary

army (AR-mee) a group of people who have been trained to fight

cannon (KAN-uhn) a large, heavy gun usually mounted on wheels

catapults (KAT-uh-*puhlts*) ancient devices used to hurl large rocks

chapel (CHAP-uhl) a building or place for prayer

destiny (DESS-tuh-nee) something that has been decided beforehand

extinct (ek-STINGKT) when something is unlikely to erupt again

fierce (FIHRSS) violent or dangerous

fortress (FOR-triss) a strong building from which people can defend an area

gunners (GUHN-erz) people who operate guns

historians (his-TOR-ree-uhnz) people who study past events

kilts (KILTS) knee-length skirts worn by Scottish men

legend (LEJ-uhnd) a story handed down from long ago that is often based on some facts but cannot be proven true

lore (LOR) knowledge learned through study

parliament (PAR-luh-muhnt) a group of people who have been elected to make laws in some countries such as the United Kingdom

peasants (PEZ-uhnts) poor farmers

scale (SKALE) climb a steep wall

scepter (SEP-tur) a staff carried by a king or queen

shift (SHIFT) a set period of time in which a person works

siege (SEEJ) an attack on a castle that lasts for a long time

soldier (SOLE-jur) a person in the army

stake (STAYK) a thick, pointed piece of wood or metal

Bibliography

Hardie, Alastair M.R. *Edinburgh's Castle in the Air.* London: Serendipity (2004).

Johnson, Paul. *Castles of England, Scotland, and Wales.* New York: HarperCollins (1989).

Tabraham, Chris. *Edinburgh Castle: The Official Souvenir Guide.* Edinburgh, Scotland: Historic Scotland (2003).

Read More

Cox, Phil Roxbee. *What Were Castles For?* Tulsa, OK: Educational Development Corporation (2002).

Jarvie, Gordon. *Scottish Castles.* Edinburgh, Scotland: National Museums of Scotland (1995).

Mackay, John, R. Ogilvie, and Kenneth Laird. *Edinburgh Castle Stories of Horror and Adventure.* Glasgow, Scotland: Lang Syne Publishers (1990).

Learn More Online

Visit these Web sites to learn more about Edinburgh Castle:

www.castlexplorer.co.uk/

www.edinburghcastle.biz/

Index

About the Author

Barbara Knox has written about Dracula's Castle in Romania,
Hearst Castle in America, and China's Forbidden City.
She lives in Minneapolis, Minnesota, with her daughter, Annie.